Rural Ecologies

A Haiku Collection

Michael J. Leach

in case of emergency press

We are proud to acknowledge the Traditional Owners of country throughout Australia and to recognise their continuing connection to land, waters, and culture.

We pay our respects to their Elders.

We support recognition, reconciliation, and reparation.

in case of emergency press

https://icoe.com.au

Rural Ecologies

A Haiku Collection

Michael J. Leach

Published by In Case of Emergency Press 2024

Copyright 2024 © Michael J. Leach

All rights reserved. Without limiting the rights under copyright reserved above, no part of this publication may be reproduced, stored in or introduced into a database and retrieval system or transmitted in any form or any means (electronic, mechanical, photocopying, recording or otherwise) without the prior written permission of both the owner of copyright and the above publishers.

ISBN: 978-0-6486111-2-7

Photograph *Wattle against Ironbark* and photograph of the author: **Irina Frolova**

Acknowledgements

The author wrote the poetry in this collection while living on the unceded land of the Dja Dja Wurrung People.

Certain haiku in this collection were first published (some with slightly different wording) across the following outlets:

Windfall: Australian Haiku, *Families, Systems, & Health* (US), *Spillwords* (US), *Live Encounters Poetry & Writing* (Indonesia), *Stereo Stories*, *Rural Fiction Magazine* (US), *Partyline*, *50 Haikus* (US), *Jalmurra* (US), and *GRAVITON* (US).

For Irina

Rural Ecologies
A *Haiku Collection*

Michael J. Leach

far corner

of the dining room—

peace lily

        hospital carpark—

        dawn light through gumtrees

        on the morning Mum passed

dirt path

to the graveyard—

Whirrakee wattle

gumtree's shadow—

Mum's grave

beside her parents'

New Year's Day

my late mother's ginger plant

flowers

sister's delayed wedding

day

autumn leaves

colour trees, air, earth

red maple

in midwinter—

two leaves left

garden bed

by the blue lake—

red-and-green kangaroo

paw

art gallery

window—

reflected gumtrees

the church

courtyard's sparse lawn—

four-leaf clover

        my guide & I cross

        lush fields lit by afternoon sun—

        my hand finds hers

we walk hand in hand—

wildflowers grow

over old train tracks

midmorning sun

through the flame tree—

we relish bagels

        sixteen red roses—

        the first time we say

        three short words

we pull in

at our remote retreat—

gymea lilies

creekside—

river red gums

creak

perched

on a river red gum branch—

the Aussie wood duck

goes *gnaarrk*

the creek's surface

ripples

round a platypus

lakeside at twilight—

water

rats

        hot night—

        fruit

        bats swoop to skim the lake

leaf

-less elm tree—

grey-headed flying foxes

hang from twigs

soccer field

at my uni campus—

grey roos

country roadside—

the motorist holds a blanket

round a joey

Tassie devil enclosure—

black eyes, nose & fur gleam

in darkness

Rural Ecologies

I drive through the bush—

      an echidna

crosses the highway

          we stretch our legs

          on the bush track—

          an echidna forms a ball

I tell a joke

to the walking group—

only kookaburras laugh

the burnt gumtree's

bifurcated branches—

koala

borrowed gumboots

I shadow the vet

as she numbs the horse's flank

Yellowstone on Stan

my cavoodle growls & barks

at all the horses

Rural Ecologies

I return—

her tuxedo cat rests

on my garment bag

        we kiss

        in the nocturnal house—

        sugar gliders

side by side

on power lines—

one possum & one magpie

Rural Ecologies

mid-walk, we spot

eastern rosellas—

stillness

blinds open—

honeyeaters in the birdbath

socialise

orchard netting—

a noisy miner flies forth

& back inside

lunchtime stroll

swift parrots in the bottlebrush

sing out *chit chit*

                display case—

                glass medicine bottles

                branded with parrots

I photograph

the shark tower—

a seagull photobombs

Anzac Day

the black swan's bugle

        nearshore—

        two black swans tend their nest

        while two cygnets float

        past

she points out words

carved on the boardwalk's handrails...

poem on black swans

we wake amidst treetops

& open blinds—

two rainbow lorikeets

                    wetland

                    encroached by buildings—

                    the pobblebonk of eastern banjo

                    frogs

sun-kissed orchard

cane borers' antennae brush

blackberry hairs

sugar bowl on the countertop—ants

        I pull up at home—

             a snail rides

        the roller door

I look out

the lounge room window—

undersides of snails

trek to the waterfall—

she pulls a leech off my ankle

with bare hands

rustling—

a lace monitor climbs

over the window pane

check-out time—

a rooster struts to our door

then crows

About the Author

Michael J. Leach lives on unceded Dja Dja Wurrung Country in his birthplace: the regional centre of Bendigo in Victoria, Australia. He acknowledges the Traditional Custodians of the land.

Michael is a poet, critic and academic who works at the Monash University School of Rural Health. Michael's poems have appeared in journals such as *Cordite* and *Plumwood Mountain*, exhibitions such as the City of Greater Bendigo's *Co.Lab* exhibitions, anthologies such as *under the same moon: Fourth Australian Haiku Anthology* (Forty South Publishing Pty Ltd, 2023), and his two previously published poetry books: the chapbook *Chronicity* (Melbourne Poets Union, 2020) and the full-length collection *Natural Philosophies* (Recent Work Press, 2022). Michael has won the UniSA Mental Health and Wellbeing Poetry Competition (2015), been a finalist in the Antarctic Poetry Exhibition Competition (2019), received a commendation in the Hippocrates Prize for Poetry and Medicine (2021), jointly won the poetry category of the Minds Shine Bright Confidence Writing Competition (2022), and been shortlisted in the poetry category of the Woollahra Digital Literary Award (2023).

Michael's next full-length poetry collection, *Chords in the Soundscapes*, is forthcoming from Ginninderra Press.

www.ingramcontent.com/pod-product-compliance
Lightning Source LLC
Chambersburg PA
CBHW032338300426
44109CB00041B/1283